Chapter 1
Who is Your Superhero?

Born and raised in Virginia, as a child I remember watching superheroes on TV and thinking one day I could fly around and save the world.

My favorite superhero was Wonder Woman. She was beautiful, strong, smart, and she could change into her outfit by simply spinning around. Most girls who loved her in those days were inspired by her just because she could fight and conquer super villains and look cute while she was doing it.

Watching her on Saturday mornings, I was empowered and had the confidence to fly just like Wonder Woman, at least in my mind. I can remember tying a long bath towel around my neck—that was my cape, and then wrapping a wide cloth hair band around my forehead, trying to look like Wonder Woman.

I would run through the house as if I was flying. Sometimes I would jump off of the back porch just to try and get the real effect of flying.

At the time I did not know that I was gaining confidence and feeling empowered to do things. All I knew was that I could accomplish anything that I needed to accomplish while pretending to be Wonder Woman. I was inspired by a fictional character and didn't really know it.

My childhood to others may be a fantasy or not, but it was all I knew. I lived in a small country town in Virginia in a middle class family. It wasn't quite as big as Mayberry on the Andy Griffin show.

I played outside, explored the forest, picked blackberries, and went to church every Sunday. I don't remember having any major life challenges as a child; therefore, I can't describe any.

As I became older I began to see the world in a different light and began to face challenges, not because my mother and father told me about them, but because of how I was treated and what I saw happening around me.

I remember going into a store to buy candy and the store clerk followed me around the store, thinking I was going to steal.

I remember in grade school being treated differently because I was African American. My classmate told me one day that black people, referring to African Americans, were dirty and asked me, "Why aren't you dirty?" I didn't respond because I couldn't understand why she felt that way. Did somebody tell her this?

I was a loner in school because I was different. I was the only African American female in my entire grade at school, and I adapted to this by entertaining myself and fantasizing about who I was going to become one day. I remember to this day how those negative experiences made me feel.

I felt less than non-minorities with whom I was in class. I couldn't understand why God would put us here all together and favor one race over another. At that time, I believed that.

So sometimes I would entertain myself and get caught up into being fictional characters because they didn't show any difference. They saved everybody from danger, making the world a better place in which to live.

Over the years, many fictional superheroes, both men and women, have come and gone. Their purpose was to bring peace and safety to people. In my personal life, my superheroes were my mother and father.

My mother worked a full-time job at a major name brand sewing factory; later she became a beautician. My mother also cooked, cleaned the house, managed five children, and always had time to show love toward us.

My mother was and still is beautiful and smart, just like Wonder Woman. She always told us that if we worked hard in life we could reach our dreams.

She also told us about challenges that we might face in life. She explained to us that because we are a minority, we have to work harder than non-minorities because nothing is given to us.

I have learned over the years from working in different organizations, that this is a true statement. It is not limited to race, but it may also apply to gender, disability, religion, etc. Some non-minority leaders only afford opportunities to others who look or act like them.

As a minority, I have to continue to work harder to prove that I am competent, and, in addition to that, if I want to be even at the same level as non-minorities in the organization, I have to possess more credentials or more validation of my skills and abilities.

My mother is my hero because she has an inner strength that gives her the ability to persevere through life challenges, never giving up. My late father worked a fulltime job, as well. He also helped my mother with the chores around the house to include maintaining our huge yard.

My father was tall and strong. When I was a small child, he would lift me high in the air. I felt safe and loved. My father worked in a plant and always told us girls that he didn't want us working in a compressor plant; he wanted us working in an office, an easy job.

My father would always say to me that girls do house work and boys do yard work. He didn't want us girls doing hard labor because he wanted us to someday have children. He believed that hard labor would physically affect us in having children.

So that's how it was at my house. My sister and I cleaned the house, and after we reached a certain age, we cooked our family meals, as well. My brothers worked in the yard.

My father was and still is my hero because he provided structure for our family. He instilled in us that we are accountable for everything that we do. He wanted us to have more in life than what he had obtained.

Even though he worked in a plant, he carried his brief case around as if he ran a major corporation, and I suppose running his household somehow equated to a major corporation. He was our leader in the home.

My late maternal grandmother was amazing! She and granddaddy had 12 children. I never knew granddaddy as he died before I was born, and I have only seen one picture of him.

My grandmother was disabled, having only one leg and a peg leg made out of wood. She lost her leg as a child by falling on a corn stalk which caused her leg to be amputated. She did not let this disability stop her.

She worked a fulltime job as a nurse and midwife for a doctor and trained her children to manage the house and farm while she cooked, cleaned, and cared for the children of the doctor.

Many times my grandmother sacrificed being with her family because she had to work; she wanted to make sure she provided for her family.

She was and is still my hero because she proved that a disability doesn't have to stop a person from having a fulfilling life. If she could do all that she did, I can do what I need to do to accomplish my goals.

My grandmother loved her family. She was a Christian woman who instilled strong religious values in her family and the generations that followed.

I was raised to understand that my role as a woman was to cook, clean, and manage children while working a 40-plus hour week.

My sister and I were taught at an early age that when we were married, we were to serve our husbands in our homes, ensuring that dinner was ready and that he came from work to a clean house even after we had worked a full day.

I believe women who are performing this role in their homes with or without husbands, are superheroes.

In grade school my superhero was my kindergarten teacher. She was a Caucasian lady. We didn't have African American teachers for many years at my school. So at that time I couldn't really identify with a role model who looked like me in elementary school.

My teacher was really, really old with gray curly hair. She was so sweet to me.

I remember one day at lunch I had fallen asleep face down in my plate. She woke me and cleaned me up. My classmates laughed at me, but she quickly silenced their laughter.

That day I learned that she was my protector at school and that she wanted me to do well in school. I always walked ahead of the class line with my kindergarten teacher.

She kept me safe from others who would have unintentionally stifled the development of my self-confidence. Even at the age of five, I identified with someone whose purpose was to guide me and teach me.

Sometimes fictional superheroes keep others safe by conquering super villains just as my teacher did for me. I believe that in life all of us have to, at some point, face super villains or adverse situations.

Super villains may be in our schools, at our jobs, at the mall, or in another vehicle, and sometimes they are disguised—we just don't really know who they are.

Society has depicted fictional superheroes as leaders because of their roles in saving people from danger and making the world a better place in which to live.

As women we are first leaders in our homes, and then we are leaders in the workplace. At home, we keep our children safe.

We inspire confidence in our children. We guide them in the right direction in life, teaching them independence, good ethics, and good morals. We develop our children into people who will one day be leaders in society. We may be raising the next President of the United States!

As leaders in the workplace, women tend to be the nurturing type. It is natural for most women because of our roles in the home.

In separate studies, Bruckmuller and Branscombe (2010) and McKinsey & Company (2009) reported that women leaders are able to handle a crisis better than men just because of their attributes and behaviors that are more conducive in navigating the crisis.

I'm not going to discuss gender differences because we all have positive attributes that we bring to society. However, women definitely have positive attributes that are needed in the workplace.

All women need that confidence to excel in the workplace. We need to discover what inspires or motivates us to be the women we desire to be, accomplishing our goals along the way.

I believe that being a superhero is not about the fictional character. It is about finding your inner strength and confidence to be able to conquer life challenges.

Identifying your superheroes is just a way of identifying your support system that gets you through life challenges, motivating and inspiring you and bringing to the surface abilities you did not know you had.

Chapter 2
Take Time to Wash Your "Superhero" Cape

As women, most of the time in addition to taking care of the children, cooking, and cleaning, we must also do the laundry. When our clothes get dirty, we have to wash them in order to have a fresh set of clothes to wear.

Our clothes are sometimes dirty because we have done physical work in them, causing them to smell and become dirty. If I was to clean my house all day without stopping, it might cause me to become tired and dirty from all of the scrubbing of the bathrooms, floors, and furnishings.

Metaphorically, a dirty or worn-out cape may be a sign that you are tired and that you may have exhausted your ability to accomplish your goals. We all know by now that in our minds, metaphorically, we each have our own superhero capes.

Life can be challenging and may affect our bodies, mentally and physically. Every once in a while we need to wash our capes in the sense that we need to take them off because we don't really need to be flying with a dirty cape.

Sometimes when we try to accomplish goals, but we are too tired, we are wasting our time and just really need to rest and refresh.

We wash our clothes because when we put on clean clothes that smell great and are unwrinkled, we feel good about ourselves and are able to function more effectively, especially when we know that others are looking at us.

When I am feeling good about myself, I am able to accomplish more goals or tasks. Life experiences can take a lot out of a person. This is the time to refresh and rest.

Maybe go to a movie, attend a party, read a book, soak your feet, get your nails done, get your hair done, get a massage, go on a date, go skating, go swimming, take an exercise class, go to the park by yourself and enjoy the scenery, take a vacation, or focus on your health.

Studies show that a person's emotional state improves with physical activity, causing positive emotions, improving mental health, and leading to important life outcomes (Hogan, Catalino, Mata, & Fredrickson, 2015).

The Florida Hospital reported in 2014 that rest is essential for overall health and contended that when people are rested, their memory improves, they maintain a healthy weight, their heart is healthier because they are getting more sleep, and stress is reduced.

So add some white space in your calendar occasionally, take a day of rest out of your hectic schedule, and enjoy the pleasures of life.

It is important to be happy and pamper yourself according to what you believe will reenergize you for the continuation of your flight to reach your goals, your destination.

Reenergization benefits everyone around you. When you are happy, your family is happy, and others with whom you are in contact are happy.

Pampering is essential in that it assists with the confidence we need while we are obtaining our goals, during our flight toward success.

As women we go through different seasons in our lives. Your seasons began when you learned how to eat, talk, and walk, from your first day of school, meeting new friends, going to parties, understanding why we have menstrual cycles, graduating from high school, learning how to cook, learning how to clean, getting your first job, going to college, joining the military, having sex for the first time, falling in love, being rejected by others, getting married, being single, getting a divorce, having your first baby, losing a child, being a soccer mom, experiencing the rebellion of a teenager, menopause, hair turning gray, wrinkles appearing, and seeing your loved ones die. These are just some examples of seasons a woman may experience.

"When it is time for a season to change, the imperfections of life are most visible" (Detweiler, 2017). Each season comes in its own time, representing a period in your life in which you are growing and developing into strong women who lead others in life.

Going through these seasons can be stressful, and learning how to love and pamper yourself is essential. It is important to recognize how to progress through the seasons by learning and recognizing your successes and failures in each season.

As grown women we do have responsibilities that require us to be present mentally and physically, and to better accomplish these responsibilities we should take time to relax and refresh. I asked some of my friends, "How do you relax and refresh?"

One friend told me she took weekend trips by herself to a hotel, enjoying the amenities of the hotel to the fullest. Another friend said she went for long drives out in the country.

Another friend said she attended church more often to experience the peace and spirituality. Another friend believed that painting pretty pictures took her away from everyday life challenges.

My cousin believes that when she shops for her clothes, it relaxes her, and the clothes that she buys give her confidence because she feels that she looks good and when she goes to work she can accomplish any task. She believes she can do anything just like when I put my cape on as a child and I believed I could do anything!

Have you ever heard the saying that you need to dress, not for your current job, but for the job you want?

Years ago when I was in my early twenties, I worked at a temporary job service. Most of the jobs that I was assigned were office jobs. I always dressed professionally in dress suits. It didn't matter if I was a data entry clerk, a phone operator, or a payroll clerk; I wore a suit.

I was dressing how I wanted others to see me: a young professional woman. I wanted to someday wear the suit aligned with the title of accomplishment. It was much more than just wearing a suit. It was where I wanted to be in my professional life.

According to etiquette expert Jacqueline Whitmore, your "clothing makes a statement about who you are and where you want to go" (Fisher, 2015).

Feeling good about yourself in how you look in your eyes and in the eyes of others gives you confidence, allowing you to present yourself in a positive way so that people will listen to you and your ideas.

After you are pampered and rested, put your cape back on and get back on course; take flight! Success comes from within. Taking care of yourself first is essential before you can take care of others or accomplish your goals in life. It's about changing your mindset. See yourself doing it, feel yourself doing it, walk in it!

Words are things too, so be careful what you speak. Speak only positive things into existence, but while you are speaking it, work it. Do what you have to do to make it happen. In the Bible, James 2:26 states, "Faith without works is dead" (KJV).

So if you have faith, that means that you trust that whatever you want will happen, and if you put in the work, you will accomplish your goals. Believe it and achieve it!

I have heard people say, "Feed your focus, and starve your distractions." Therefore stay focused and use resources to find out how to do things to get you where you need to go.

The internet has a wealth of information. Go to the library, talk to people, and ask them questions. Be aware of others or things that distract you from accomplishing your goals and know that you need to back off and remain focused on your goals.

Find what you love to do. You will be great at the things about which you are passionate. Your passion, followed by confidence, fuels your flight to greatness!

Chapter 3
Women Flying as Leaders

As a child I went to Bible camp every year. Bible camp was exciting because we did arts and crafts, and I also learned about the many different stories in the Bible.

One of the stories I remember was about Adam and Eve. This story was about the beginning of humans on earth. God formed man from the dirt and then breathed into his nostrils to give him life.

He placed Adam in the Garden of Eden, giving him dominion over every living
thing. After a while God decided to create Eve, the first woman, because he didn't want Adam to be alone.

He created Eve by putting Adam into a deep sleep, and during that sleep, God took out one of his ribs. Eve was made from Adam's rib. Eve was placed on the earth to be Adam's helper (KJV Bible). Men were made from dust, but women were made from a man's rib.

From the beginning of time, gender roles on earth have been different. Women were placed on earth by God to help men. Therefore, women were helpers, their place was in the home taking care of their families

and household chores; they obeyed their husbands, and they were submissive to their men.

Women have been locked into this role since the beginning of time. Men, on the other hand, were the heads of their households; they financially supported their families; and they were brave, strong, and masculine.

Over the years our role as a woman in the home and workplace has evolved. Years ago the families were larger. Both of my parents came from large families with 5 to 12 siblings. Most women worked in their homes, cooking, cleaning, and taking care of their children.

Before the Civil War women were expected to stay home, cook, clean, and take care of their children while men worked to support their families financially. Women were dependent on men for support and, in a sense, robbed of self-confidence. After the Civil War, women began to enter the workforce in service-type jobs.

During World War II, most of the men had to fight in the war; therefore, women were forced to take jobs that they had never performed before, jobs that were once male-dominated.

After the war the men returned home, causing the women to return to their homes to do the cooking, cleaning, and caring for the children or to continue in service-type jobs. Some women were not happy about this and wanted to continue doing jobs that were once male-dominated (Shah, 2015).

Women's opportunities to gain equality in the workplace have evolved over the years. Over the years families, too, have changed; therefore, women's roles in their homes are   different.

The feminist movement gave women a chance to enjoy life to the fullest, meaning that women had rights, and women were able to advance in their careers without being hindered or discounted, just because they were women. Today women with children are either single parents or married and sharing the parenting responsibility with a spouse.

Because of the efforts of women in the nineteenth century, today's women often work outside of the home. In some households women share the responsibility of the family and house chores with their husbands while others are headed by single mothers who handle everything themselves, holding a job, caring for their children, and managing their households.

Women should be able to make as much money as men doing the same job. Most women work outside of the home but still have to manage their household responsibilities. In today's society, married and single women have a voice and are leaders in their homes and at work.

Women   are   working more today than ever before because of current day responsibilities. Women are working in the fields of medicine, science, art, business, education, and the armed forces, to name a few areas. Women want more out of life and are working hard to obtain those goals.

Women are leaders! Women are holding top positions in companies across the United States. Let's take a look at those with whom I have identified as great women leaders.

Irene Rosenfeld began her career working in consumer research at Dancer Fitzgerald Sample advertising agency. Later she joined General Foods.

Irene Rosenfeld holds the position of Chairman and CEO of the world's second-largest food company, Kraft Foods. She formerly held the position of CEO of Frito-Lay, where she helped create healthy product choices. She also announced a new recipe for success which increased the profit for Kraft Foods.

Irene Rosenfeld has accomplished so many goals in the food industry, impacting and restructuring key businesses in the United States. In 2008 she ranked sixth on the Wall Street Journal's "50 Women to Watch" list and in 2011 she ranked tenth on Forbes "Most Powerful Women" list (Storm, 2017).

Another great leader is Carol M. Meyrowitz who began her career working as an assistant buyer at Saks. She climbed the corporate ladder developing retail brands to include TJ Maxx, Marshall's, and Home Goods into a multi-billion dollar business. She is the CEO of TJX, the leading off-price retailer of apparel and home fashions in the world (Storm, 2017).

Ursula Burns began her career at Xerox, working as a mechanical engineer intern. She worked herself up the ranks, and in 2001 she prevented the company from filing bankruptcy. She also acquired Affiliated Computer Services and its 77,000 employees, making Xerox a profitable company. Ursula Burns is the first-ever African American woman CEO of a Fortune 500 company (Storm, 2017).

And who doesn't know who Oprah Winfrey is? Oprah Winfrey began her career working at a radio station in Baltimore, Maryland where she did local news updates, called cut-ins, during *Good Morning America*. Soon she was co-host of a morning talk show called *Baltimore Is Talking*.

Years later, Oprah anchored on *A.M. Chicago* bringing up the ratings and leading to her hosting the *Oprah Winfrey Show*. She continues to make a difference in people's lives by accomplishing great things that benefit us all. Oprah Winfrey's story is a separate book by itself. This woman has inspired me so much and has helped shape who I am today.

I am more confident today because God's Word says through Christ all things are possible, and, because I see the accomplishments of Oprah Winfrey, I know that all things are possible. To see a woman in this position represents where we all can be if we want it badly enough.

These women mentioned are just a few examples of many women who are flying as superheroes. They are accomplishing goals and reaching their full potential.

Working hard pays. These women have climbed their way up the corporate ladder, and they are continuing to climb their way up the corporate ladder, representing women well and leading by example.

Be who you desire to be. Find out what your purpose is by finding out what your passion is in life. I believe God made us all differently, and the passion that you have for the things that you do well are gifts from Him, and because they are gifts from Him, they will benefit others.

Chapter 4
Finding Your Passion and
Knowing the Leader in You

In chapter 2, I mentioned that your passion followed by confidence fuels your flight to greatness, motivating you to accomplish your goals.

But how do you find your passion? How do you formulate your goals? How do you transform your passions and dreams into obtainable goals?

I found my passion by realizing what I did not enjoy. Over the years I have worked in several positions at different organizations, but I was in jobs that did not excite me at all. I dreaded going to work every day just because I knew I would be doing a job that I didn't enjoy.

Years ago I can remember leaving a job after two days just because I didn't like anything related to math. The position I left was an accounts payable job through a temporary job service.

I finally realized that in every job I've had, I have enjoyed helping others. I guess you could say I love customer service.

Later I realized that I wanted to help others become better at what they do. At that time I worked in human resources. I learned the importance of the training and development of human resources and how it improves how an organization operates.

One of my duties as a personnel assistant was the task of training employees in human resources topics. In the beginning I didn't like getting up in front of others. However, several years later I was able to do that without any fear at all.

I was able to overcome my fears because first, I recognized that public speaking made me nervous. Secondly, I researched "How to overcome the fear of public speaking."

What I learned was that if I was very knowledgeable in the topic I was presenting, I wouldn't be so fearful of speaking. I took this information and applied it to every class I had to teach, and it worked!

I also learned that if I practiced, practiced, and practiced, this would decrease fear. Guess what? It worked, too! Because I practiced so much, I gained confidence, and I became comfortable in front of others.

Other than pushing past my fears, I had to embrace my uniqueness. My uniqueness was that I have never met a stranger. My interpersonal skills are amazing! Interpersonal skills are simply how you interact with others. I created that personal connection with the attendees before the training began.

I found that my passion was what I enjoyed doing. What gives you pure joy? From experience I learned that if I wasn't good at something, it was because I wasn't passionate about it, couldn't do it, or just didn't like it.

Over the years, I have had many goals; some I have accomplished and others I have not accomplished. The point is that it's okay to discard or change your goals. Formulating your goals is simply creating a plan, a timeline to attain your goals.

The following is a plan, showing the formulation of how I

accomplished my goals:

    a. Think about where you want to be in one to five years.

    b. What do you want to achieve?

    c. What training, if any, do you need to accomplish goals?

    d. Develop specific goals that inspire and motivate you and that are important to you.

    e. Write your goals down.

    f. Have a positive attitude!

    g. Set measureable, attainable, and relevant steps to attain your goals. Write down even the smallest details if that helps.

    h. Set a deadline.

    i. Practice "Perseverance all day everyday!"

This plan allowed me to discover what I wanted to accomplish, not what mom or dad, friends, or co-workers wanted for me. Honing down my passions and dreams was simply perfecting what I do well, putting me in a position to accomplish my goals or dreams.

I became a public speaker because I learned my craft, and I continue to develop my craft by researching, attending conferences, and taking classes that provide knowledge that adds value to my personal and professional life, shaping who I am today: a leader who is in flight!

I believe that before you can lead others, you have to manage yourself and know who you are as a leader. One important task in leading by example is the act of reflection.

Reflection should be something that is practiced on a regular basis. This will assist in your progression into an effective leader.

Reflect on the areas of how others perceive you and how you see yourself. Also be aware of your emotions and other interpersonal skills needed for effective leadership.

During your reflection you may ask yourself these questions: Am I walking uprightly? Meaning, are you doing the right thing in front of others and while you are alone?

If the morals and values exhibited by the culture within your organization don't align with your own morals and values, consider finding another organization for which to work.

Am I transforming others from their current state of thinking or acting, to
a better state of thinking or acting?

To transform others as a leader is to provide others with the resources needed for accomplishment. A transformational leader is one who delegates and develops the followers' skills and self-confidence.

Using this style of leadership with your interpersonal skill of communication may result in conflict resolution, understanding a task, or simply developing effective relationships.

Transformational leaders lead by clearly communicating valuable information to gain commitment from others. They are able to do so through personal identification and involvement.

Transformational leaders motivate others to work toward goals that go beyond immediate self-interest. Transformational leaders are positive, strong, and committed to goal attainment (Abdul & Javed, 2012).

Other questions you may want to ask yourself are the following: Am I using effective communication by listening and providing feedback? Am I approachable? Do I really care about others being successful? Do I lead by example? Do I practice emotional intelligence?

Emotional intelligence is simply being aware of your emotions and the emotions of others before you approach the person or situation. This will better assist with how to approach others or situations, guiding your actions.

Interpersonal skills assist with developing positive relationships thereby influencing and leading others toward success.

As leaders we should have the ability to influence others to attain goals. You influence others by simply using your style of leadership, with your interpersonal skills, in a positive way.

It is important that we, as role models or leaders to our women, develop effective relationships with them. This provides support to them and gives them the confidence to be leaders themselves and inspire them to "fly!"

Chapter 5
Inspiring Others to Fly

The ability to uplift others with our words and actions is how we inspire others. Everything that we say and do reflects who we are. We want to inspire and encourage others to excel in life. We are role models without choice and should act accordingly.

Society has changed in how the media portrays women, specifically minorities, on some reality shows, bringing dangerous stereotypes to our homes.

It is not okay to swear and be disrespectful to others. It is not okay to allow men to disrespect you. It is not okay to keep having babies for a paycheck.

It is not okay to use men for money. It is not okay for you to allow men to use you sexually. These types of behaviors portrayed by the media are mentally and emotionally hurting our young women.

The drama, sex, and material things have drawn women to these types of shows, causing them to think that maybe all they need to do is find a man in the entertainment business or sports world, or maybe all they need to do is get pregnant so that they themselves can be part of a reality show.

The reality show, *Teen Mom*, is a show about young mothers struggling to raise a baby while they are still in school, and some may view this show as an inspiration to other moms in similar situations, while others may view this show as a way to further promote teen pregnancy.

Another reality show, *Bad Girls Club*, depicts young women as binge drinking party animals who are constantly causing drama and fighting (Smith, 2014).

Should we continue to allow the promotion of such negative stereotypes? I watched one of the reality shows one night and found it very shaming to women in regards to how they presented themselves.

On this particular show the women, maybe four or five, were at a restaurant eating. They were very beautiful women; however, when they spoke, trash came out. They had nothing of substance to say. The luncheon ended in an argument.

I was very disappointed because I knew that my daughter was watching this show. As older women we should watch everything that we say and do because younger women are using us as their role models. We must lead by example.

We should want to lead our young women toward a positive future, trying to eliminate the challenges that they may face during their journeys in life. Our young girls and young women need positive role models.

Our responsibility is to guide youth in a direction that will give them the confidence to achieve goals without dependence on others or the false realities of society that television has portrayed.

Recently I had a discussion with my 23-year-old daughter. I asked her why she enjoys watching the reality shows.

She said she likes the drama, such as fighting over men, swearing, disrespecting others, and other less than uplifting behaviors. Her friends, male and female, also enjoy the drama of reality shows.

Negative societal influences are just ways of degrading women, causing them to believe in false realities that are not adding any value to their lives.

To influence my daughter I needed to first understand why she enjoyed the shows, and then I needed to see if the actions of the reality stars were affecting her.

From a personal experience, I discovered that the negativity in the reality shows she was watching was affecting the actions of my daughter.

At one point, when she was younger, she told me that she wanted to be a basketball wife. I don't know if she was serious or if she was just trying to get under my skin because I didn't really allow her to watch those types of shows. My fear was that my daughter was viewing her womanhood as a way to get things.

As women we want to accomplish goals through merit, working hard for what we have. My job as a parent was to change her mindset of how she viewed women and women's roles to a more positive mindset, showing her that women are strong, intelligent, and caring, having so much to add to their lives and the lives of others than what is shown on reality shows.

As a child I always pictured myself in front of thousands of people. Some members of my family say that because my birth sign is a Leo, I just want to get attention. I'm not an advocate of horoscope signs; however, I do believe that my personality matches the description of a Leo exactly.

I desired to be in front of people because I believed I could sing. I wish that years ago we'd had reality type talent shows like *American Idol* or the *X-Factor* that showcase true talent.

These types of talent shows inspire people of all ages to share their gifts of singing with others. The judges provide constructive feedback to them in hopes of improving their musical talent.

Another positive reality show is *The Biggest Loser*. This show is one of my favorites because it is a show   about people who have weight loss challenges. It shows the obstacles they must overcome in their quest to get healthy.

This show is an inspiration to others who are going through the same experience. Positive or negative, reality shows can be educational, and we will learn something from them.

As leaders, role models, and women, we help others by walking, speaking, and presenting ourselves in a manner that people will want to follow based on our actions and how we treat them.

Leaders have the ability to influence others to attain goals. Having a positive influence on others ensures that they are on the path toward success.

Guiding women toward goal accomplishment is important. This will inspire them and give them the confidence needed to get them through life challenges. A way to inspire others is through mentoring.

Mentoring can and should be used to guide others toward success. Mentoring is a one-on-one relationship between a person who acts as a guide or advisor and an individual who is younger or less experienced.

Augustine (2014) stated that mentoring is a non-parental relationship with a younger person, in which the mentor acts in a caring and supportive way.

Mentoring is a developmental, sharing, caring relationship where a person invests his or her time, knowledge, and efforts in enhancing another person's growth. Developing effective mentoring relationships will inspire mentees to follow you as a leader in their lives.

Recently I had the pleasure of speaking before a group of young mothers, ages 16 to
to 21. Upon my arrival to their group home, the young women were sizing me up from head to toe and even made a few remarks as if I wasn't present.

I have to admit that the beginning was rough, but slowly they warmed up to me by participating in the discussion; therefore, when I began to speak, they seemed to be listening to what I had to share.

My presentation was about securing your cape, developing life goals, and how to attain them. I mentioned that as women we have many responsibilities in life, and we have to work hard to become successful.

I also mentioned to them that even though they are faced with life challenges, they need to face those challenges by resolving them, bringing to surface underlying issues. These young women needed to understand that they could fly through their storms, their challenges.

One young lady mentioned that they were tired of speakers coming and telling them sad stories, so I explained to them that sometimes when people become successful, they have had to experience difficult things that eventually paved their way to success.

I told them that sometimes in life we have to experience sadness because we learn from it, and it shapes who we are and guides or motivates us to accomplish goals or to go where we want to go in life.

At the end of my presentation the young women worked on vision boards that were colored either blue or red in the shapes of superhero capes.

Each cape had a ribbon at the top where they tied their capes, securing their capes for flight. They were able to paste pictures of where they wanted to be in life and pictures of how to get there.

I explained to them that although as women we have many responsibilities, we still have to strive to accomplish our personal goals. We must keep flying even though we run into rainclouds or storms.

I hope that I was able to inspire the young ladies that day because they most definitely inspired me.

This experience led me to listen more to what youth are saying and try to understand that they are growing up in a different era than the era in which I grew up. The challenges that I had to face at that age are different from the challenges they have to face.

I believe that life experiences shape who you are as an individual, and the experience that I had with them most definitely has added value to my life. I left their home with pure joy in my heart!

are the obstacles or challenges that will soon pass, so women, secure your cape and visualize your goals or destination! You have so much more flying to do!

Over the years I have worked several places all over the world. One place in particular was at a highly recognized, national organization. I remember when I first received the job offer to work there I was so excited!

After I started working there, I noticed that the majority of the workforce was made up of Caucasian males. Not many women were in leadership roles and few minorities were employed. However, I was hired to do a job, and I was there to do my best!

At the very beginning of working at this organization I immediately noticed that my supervisor, a Caucasian male, was checking every day to see if I was on time and how long I took my breaks.

His behavior did not seem strange at first. I figured because I was a new employee, he needed to learn what my work habits were. However, his behavior continued.

Months later during a meeting with him, I jokingly mentioned his surveillance type activities. He laughed and indicated to me that the lady who had previously held my position was African American, and she drove the same type of car as I did.

He proceeded to explain that she never was on time, took long lunch breaks, and didn't really do a good job. He thought that because she was African American and I was African American that we might act the same way.

I was really surprised at this; therefore, I set out to change how he perceived minority women. His propensity to trust me was low due to his past experience.

Over the years I was able to gain his trust and hopefully change his perception of minorities. He was one of the best supervisors I have ever had.

I believe that when we started to communicate that day and
continued   effective communication, he began to see who I was

as a person and as an employee.

While I was working at this organization, I completed both my Master's degree and my Doctoral degree.

Because I was working hard at improving professionally, I believed that I could hold a leadership position. However, the closer I came to completing my doctoral degree, the more challenging I found my situation to be.

It was challenging because I believed that some people who were part of leadership didn't want to see me successful. I believed that they still saw me as an assistant, my first job there.

After I received a promotion, I later was asked to develop leadership courses for the organization, a position I gladly accepted.

One individual was not happy with this decision and was determined to destroy my career. This individual was a Caucasian female. She was in a leadership role at this organization. She asked my supervisor to demote me.

At the time she constantly talked about me to others, and because she was in a high leadership role, she stopped my promotions by telling lies about me and my work ethic, convincing others that I was incompetent. She told me I was arrogant because of how I walked and spoke.

I don't believe that to be true. I believe that I am confident, and when I speak I am professional in my manner. In addition, she made a comment about how she wanted someone who looked like leadership in front of leadership.

When someone makes this type of statement, it clearly indicates that minorities are not desired for training or teaching leadership at an organization dominated by Caucasian males.

Time and time again I ignored this individual and continued to let my work speak for itself. It seemed like the more praise I received from others, the more obsessed she was with my daily activities.

After meeting with her and trying to resolve the issues, I came to the conclusion that this individual was insecure, threatened by my accomplishments.

To overcome this challenge, I decided not to allow this toxic individual to drag me down. I decided to stand up and use the negative situation to motivate me to prove, not to her, but to myself that I am worthy of everything for which I have worked.

Therefore, the more obsessed she became, the more motivated I was to complete my doctorate degree.

I eventually asked to be moved to another department, not because I was running away, but because I love who I am and I needed peace to fulfill my purpose in life.

So I truly thank this individual because she was and still is one of my motivators to succeed. This place was a very challenging place to work, and because of the challenges that I faced and overcame, I am a stronger person!

My past experiences have inspired me to share them with you, so that you will not have to go through the same types of experiences.

Don't ever let anyone tell you or suggest to you that you can't achieve your goals. Don't ever let someone make you stress to the point you become ill. Don't ever to allow someone to discount your skills and abilities.

In my mind, this one individual at this one organization equated to a fictional villain. We all have fictional villains or life challenges. The key to success is overcoming the villains or situations by facing them.

Many processes have been written about and published that will give step-by-step instructions on how to handle difficult people. Difficult people and challenges are everywhere we go.

However, I faced this villain and conquered by not stepping outside of my character and simply by facing the situation and maintaining my professionalism.

Another way to conquer a villain in your life is to stay focused on your goals and purpose in life. Follow the advice of our former First Lady Michelle Obama: "When they go low, we go high."

Be the bigger person, continue to show them the undeserved

respect, and show them that you will do well in life regardless of their many attempts to stop you. Use villains or anyone who is trying to stifle your progress as motivators to do well in life.

Challenges in our world may be equated to the fictional world when superheroes are flying high and they run into rainclouds, storms, hurricanes, tornados, or other inclement weather. Those superheroes figured out a way to get through the difficult raincloud or situation, and so can you!

As women we secretly wear superhero capes, and we may face the rainclouds or challenges in our lives, but stay strong and persevere all day every day. Secure your cape and fly through bad weather. We have goals to accomplish!

Chapter 7
Reaching Your Destination

It is in your destination where you will find a sense of joy, accomplishment, completeness, and peace. Your destination may be connected to your spirituality. I believe that God made us to fulfill a purpose, and anything at which we are good is our gift from Him.

God is inside of me; therefore, victory is in me, power is in me, anointing is in me, joy is in me, imagination is in me, and creativity is in me. All of these gifts from God assist with attaining our goals. Be who God designed you to be!

How and when you reach your destination is all in your control. The decisions you make during your flight may cause you to lose altitude.

This is when the storms come that you have to face or challenges arise that you need to overcome. Gaining altitude is based on your positive actions that result in accomplishing your goals, getting you back in flight above the horizon.

Reaching your destination does not mean that you stop flying. It simply means that you have accomplished a goal, and now you need to accomplish another one by taking another flight.

Determine what your new direction or destination will be. Continue to set personal and professional goals for yourself.

When I think about the women who have reached their destination, I think of successful women, women who have changed history and who have paved the way for us today.

I praise God for Helena Rubinstein, an American business woman who established one of the world's first cosmetic companies. Sometimes wearing makeup gives me confidence because I believe I am looking good. When I am in this state of mind, I believe I can do anything!

Madam C. J. Walker developed hair-care products for African American women (Learning English, 2007).

Personally, this one invention alone can preach! When my hair is looking good, I know it, and I can focus on accomplishing goals in my life. Again, women have confidence when they look and feel good.

I am not saying that our outside appearance defines who we are because it doesn't. However, it is the way that we feel which motivates us to act in a certain way. If I am looking and dressing like the president of a company, I am either the president or I'm going to be the president one day!

Eleanor Roosevelt, wife of President Franklin D. Roosevelt, made a significant contribution to the 1948 United Nations declaration of human rights.

Sojourner Truth, an African-American women's rights campaigner, was known for her famous extemporaneous speech "Ain't I a Woman?" which depicted how women are equal to men (Biography Online, 2017).

Many women have made differences in how we see ourselves and how the world now perceives us. To them I would like to say thank you. We greatly appreciate your hard work and efforts in solidifying who we really are as women. We are strong, we are beautiful, and we are intelligent.

Women are the life lines for human beings. We are all heroes to someone, but we have to continue to make differences in our world, so secure your cape because we have so much more flying to do!

Others need you to inspire them. Reflect on your journey thus far. Determine who your superheroes have been. What added value have they brought to your life?

Conclusion

Women are mothers, wives, sisters, friends, teachers, pastors, and much more. To simply put it, women are leaders. We are leaders in our homes, at our jobs, and, really, everywhere we go.

Women are confident and powerful! We can do anything that we want to do in life. We are here to inspire, motivate, and encourage others to be successful. We are role models, not by choice, but by our roles in society and what society expects us to be.

Take that role proudly, women. You are raising children. Whether you are a mother or not, you have had an influence in a child's life. These children are growing up to be nurses, doctors, teachers, secretaries, and others who impact our world. These children will soon be running our country.

Know who you are and who you are to the world. Why not? Oprah knows who she is. She has said, "I was once afraid of people saying, 'Who does she think she is?' Now I have the courage to stand and say, 'This is who I am.'"

Life isn't easy. Our life experiences shape who we are. We all have a different story or a different destination. You can't be scared to fly. If you quit, you will not reach your destination. Fly high, and let others see you fly. When others see you fly, this will inspire them to take flight.

Recently I found out that my cousin had finished her four-year degree. I didn't even know she was pursuing it. After she graduated I spoke to her, and she told me thank you for being an inspiration.

She told me that I was her inspiration to pursue her educational goals. She said she watched how I worked, raised a family, and finished my degrees, and if I could do it, she could do it. When I learned this, I was speechless. I didn't realize that I have had an effect on others like that.

When you wake up every day, envision where you're going, and do something that day that helps you get closer to your vision.

Stay focused, and, if needed, reinvent your life.

Greatness exists in all of us. Change your negatives to positives, fly through the storms so that you will see many rainbows, and see the sun shining while you're flying. You've got this!

What I would like for you to take away from this book is to understand and be proud of who you are. Don't let anyone discourage you from achieving your dreams. Be aware of how you can change the lives of others around
you.

Face your challenges and overcome them. Continue to lead by example. Be a leader to all, not just to other women. Don't give up; that is not an option. Just remember, Perseverance All DAY EVERYDAY!

References

Abdul, Q. C., & Javed, H. (2012). Impact of transactional and laissez-faire
leadership style on motivation. *International Journal of Business and Social Science, 3*(7), n/a. Retrieved from http://search.proquest.com/docvie w/1010404396?accountid=35812

Angelou, Maya, 1978. And still I rise: A book of poems. Retrieved from https://read.amazon.com/kp/embed?asin=B005EGXP7K&tag=bing08-20&linkCode=kpp&reshareId=Z7Z86XJCYZ97ETWWQ7DP&reshar

Augustine, K. A. (2014). *Teacher mentors: Lived experiences mentoring at-risk middle school students* (Doctoral Dissertation). Retrieved from ProQuest. (Order Number 3665070)

Biography Online, 2017. Women who changed the world. Retrieved from http://www.biographyonline.net/people/women-who-changed-world.html

Bruckmüller, S., and Branscombe, N. (2010). The glass cliff: When and why women are selected as leaders in crisis contexts. *The British Journal of Social Psychology, 49*(3), 433-451. Retrieved from MEDLINE database

Detweiler, S. (2017). 9 traits of a life-giving mom: Replacing my worst with God's best. Retrieved from https://www.goodreads.com/quotes/tag/seasons-of-life

Encyclopedia of World Biography, 2017. Oprah Winfrey biography. Retrieved from http://www.notablebiographies. com/We-Z/Winfrey-Oprah.html

Fisher, A. (2015). Should you still 'dress for the job you want'? Retrieved from http://fortune.com/2015/03/19/dress-job-promotions/

Hogan, C. L., Catalino, L. I., Mata, J., & Fredrickson, B. L. (2015). Beyond

emotional benefits: Physical activity
and sedentary behavior affect psychosocial resources through
emotions. *Psychology & Health, 30*(3), 354-369.
doi:10.1080/08870446.2014.973410

Learning English (2007). Madam C. J. Walker, 1867-1919: She developed
hair-care products for black women. Retrieved from
https://learningenglish.voanews.com/a/a-23-2007-01-27-voa1-
83132542/127071.html

McKinsey & Company (2009). Women matter 3: Women leaders, a
competitive edge in and after crisis. Retrieved from
http://www.mckinsey.com/search.aspx?q=women+matter+3

Shah, D. (2015). The evolution of women in the workforce (1865-2015).
Retrieved from
http://workingwomen.web.unc.edu/2015/04/23/revision-summary/

Smith, K. (2014). Despite their entertainment value, reality TV often
promotes dangerous stereotypes. Retrieved from
http://ninertimes.com/2014/04/despite-the-entertainment-value-
reality-tv-often-promotes-dangerous-stereotypes/

Storm, A. (2017). Top 10 female CEOs & influential business women of
American companies Retrieved from
http://www.moneycrashers.com/female-ceos-influential-women-
business/

The Florida Hospital (2014). State of health.
https://www.floridahospital.com/blog/health-benefits-of-rest posted
by: Andre Seballo

Whyte, G. (2015). 5 ways to overcome challenges. Retrieved from
https://www.psychologies.co.uk/5-ways-overcome-challenges